Fun Fan Facts:
The Unofficial NBA Edition

Washington Wizards

Everything Young Wizards Fans Should Know

By: Jake Liam

Dedication

To every Wizards fan who has ever sat in Capital One Arena hoping this is the year it finally clicks. You have cheered through name changes, city changes, lineup changes, and about a thousand trades that made you go "wait, we did what?" Your loyalty is genuinely impressive.

And to Washington, D.C. The city that built the nation, the Capitol, and one seriously underrated basketball franchise.

This one is for the District.

THE NBA BY THE NUMBERS

MOST NBA CHAMPIONSHIPS*

- CELTICS (18) †
- LAKERS (17)
- WARRIORS (7)
- BULLS (6)
- SPURS (5)

As of the 2024-25 Season. † One Trophy = 4 Championships.

NBA HISTORY SNAPSHOT

- **1946** NBA Founded
- **1954** Shot Clock Introduced
- **1979** 3-Point Line Added
- **2023** NBA Cup Introduced

BIG NUMBERS

$156 million
Stephen Curry's est. earnings in the 24-25 season

7'7"
Tallest player in NBA history (Gheorghe Mureșan & Manute Bol)

30 | 4 | 82

30 Teams Competing in the NBA

4 Playoff Rounds

82 Games Per Season

WASHINGTON WIZARDS
IN THE NBA

- FOUNDED: 1961 †
- NBA TITLES: 2
- CONFERENCE TITLES: 4*

40 Playoff Appearances

*† Founding dates are complicated & may cause arguments at Thanksgiving. Ask someone born before color TV. All Titles reflect pre-relocation franchise history. * As of 2024-25 Season.*

NBA ALL-TIME MVP LEADERS

KAREEM ABDUL-JABBAR (6) ★ MICHAEL JORDAN (5) ★ BILL RUSSELL (5)

EASTERN CONFERENCE

- Atlantic – **Celtics**
- Atlantic – **Nets**
- Atlantic – **Knicks**
- Atlantic – **76ers**
- Atlantic – **Raptors**
- Central – **Bulls**
- Central – **Cavaliers**
- Central – **Pistons**
- Central – **Pacers**
- Central – **Bucks**
- Southeast – **Hawks**
- Southeast – **Hornets**
- Southeast – **Heat**
- Southeast – **Magic**
- Southeast – **Wizards**

WESTERN CONFERENCE

- Pacific – **Lakers**
- Pacific – **Clippers**
- Pacific – **Warriors**
- Pacific – **Suns**
- Pacific – **Kings**
- Northwest – **Nuggets**
- Northwest – **Timberwolves**
- Northwest – **Thunder**
- Northwest – **Trail Blazers**
- Northwest – **Jazz**
- Southwest – **Mavericks**
- Southwest – **Rockets**
- Southwest – **Spurs**
- Southwest – **Pelicans**
- Southwest – **Grizzlies**

Introduction

Welcome, fans! Whether you're new to cheering for the Washington Wizards or you've been bleeding the team colors your whole life, this book is packed with fun, exciting facts about your favorite team. Get ready to impress your friends and family with everything you know about the Wizards.

Quick Timeout

This book is packed with stats. Like, A LOT of stats. Every fact was checked, double-checked, and triple-checked. But here's the thing about basketball history: not everyone agrees on everything. Ask someone who watched games before color TV and someone who grew up with instant replay and you'll get two completely different answers. My dad, stepdad, uncle, and grandpa all argued about the same fact. Four people. Four answers. All of them think they're right. So if you spot something that doesn't match what you've heard, congratulations. You might be a bigger fan than the people who helped make this book. And honestly? That's pretty cool.

HOW IT WORKS

THE SEASON

82 Games. One Goal.

Each team plays 82 games.
Win enough to make the
Playoffs.
Every game counts!

PLAYOFFS

30 Teams. 16 Make It.

8 per conference make the playoffs.
Win=Advance | Lose=Go Home
Best record
gets home court!

PLAYOFF ROUNDS

Best of 7. Win 4 or Go Home.

4 rounds of pure pressure.
Every series is do-or-die!

OVERTIME?

5 More Minutes.

Keep playing until
someone pulls ahead.
No ties. Ever.

THE FINALS

One Series. One Champion.

Winner lifts the Trophy.
Legend status unlocked.

How the NBA Works

At first glance, basketball feels simple. Ten players. One ball. Two hoops. Go.

Then the NBA adds the layers.

An 82-game regular season. A draft where bad teams pick first. Playoffs that last two full months. Superstars who can change everything with one trade. Dynasties that rise, fall, and rise again.

And somehow, it all works.

The NBA is built on one big idea: every team gets a chance to reset, reload, and rise again. No relegation. No dropping down to a lower league. Just basketball, every night, from October through June.

It is a league designed for drama, stars, and comebacks. And once you understand the flow, it is impossible to stop watching.

The League Setup

The NBA has 30 teams, spread across the United States and Canada. Those teams are split into two conferences:

- Eastern Conference
- Western Conference

Each conference has three divisions, mostly based on geography. Divisions matter for scheduling, but not as much as they used to.

Every team plays 82 regular season games, usually from October through April. Home games. Road games. Back-to-back nights. Long road trips. The season is a marathon before the sprint even starts.

Win games, and you climb the standings. Lose too many, and the pressure builds fast.

How Games Are Played

An NBA game has four quarters, each lasting 12 minutes. That means 48 minutes of game time, plus timeouts, free throws, and the occasional coach argument that adds another 20 minutes nobody planned for.

Scoring is simple:

- A shot inside the three-point line is worth 2 points
- A shot beyond the arc is worth 3 points
- Free throws are worth 1 point

If the score is tied at the end of regulation, the game goes to overtime, which lasts 5 minutes. Still tied? Another overtime. Keep going until someone wins.

There is a shot clock too. Teams have 24 seconds to take a shot. No standing around. No holding the ball forever. Keep it moving.

The Regular Season Race

The regular season is long for a reason. It tests everything.

Depth. Health. Focus. Patience.

Teams play opponents from both conferences, but they face conference rivals more often. By the end of the season, each conference's top teams have earned their playoff spots the hard way.

The goal is simple: make the playoffs. But there is a twist.

The NBA Cup

In 2023, the NBA added something new to the middle of the season. Something with actual stakes. They called it the In-Season Tournament, now known as the NBA Cup.

It works like this: Every team plays a small group stage during November and December, with special court designs that look like nothing else in basketball. The best teams advance to a knockout round held in Las Vegas.

The winners split a prize pool. Players earn bonus money. And for the first time, a team could lift a trophy before the playoffs even started.

Some fans are still warming up to it. Some players love it. But the moment a team starts treating it seriously and a crowd shows up buzzing in December, it feels like something.

Which, honestly, sounds about right.

The Play-In Tournament

Instead of sending the top eight teams from each conference straight to the playoffs, the NBA added something new. The Play-In Tournament.

Here is how it works:

- Teams ranked 1 through 6 in each conference are safe
- Teams ranked 7 through 10 fight for the final two playoff spots

The 7 and 8 seeds have an advantage. Win once and you are in. Lose and you still get one more shot. The 9 and 10 seeds have to win twice in a row just to earn a first-round matchup.

It turns the end of the season into a sprint. Every game suddenly matters more. Fans love it. Coaches age rapidly.

The NBA Playoffs

Once the playoffs begin, everything tightens.

Sixteen teams enter. Eight from each conference. Every round is a best-of-seven games series. That means the first team to win four games moves on:

- First Round
- Conference Semifinals
- Conference Finals
- NBA Finals

Home-court advantage matters. Crowds get louder. Rotations get shorter. Superstars play heavier minutes. One bad quarter can flip a series. One great performance can define a career.

By the time the NBA Finals arrive in June, only two teams are left. One from the East. One from the West. Four wins away from a championship. Four wins away from history.

The NBA Draft: Hope Begins Here

Here is where the NBA gets clever. Every summer, new players enter the league through the NBA Draft. Teams take turns selecting college players, international stars, and teenagers straight out of high school.

The teams that finished with the worst records get the best odds to pick early through the Draft Lottery. It is not guaranteed, but it gives struggling franchises a real shot at changing their future with one pick.

That means one bad season does not doom you forever. It might actually change everything. Some franchises are rebuilt by a single draft night moment.

Hope shows up wearing a new jersey.

No Relegation. All Pressure.

Unlike many global sports leagues, NBA teams never drop down to a lower league. They always stay in the NBA.

That does not mean there is no pressure.

Fans remember losing seasons. Owners make changes. Coaches get replaced. Players get traded. Every year is a test of direction, patience, and belief.

Stars, Systems, and Showtime

The NBA is famous for its stars. But stars do not win alone.

Teams need chemistry. Coaches need systems. Role players need to deliver on the biggest stages. One injury. One hot streak. One trade deadline deal. Any of it can flip a season.

That balance between individual brilliance and team basketball is what makes the league special.

Fast breaks. Buzzer-beaters. Game 7s. And moments that get replayed forever. That is the NBA.

Once you get the flow, it is pure electricity.

Washington Wizards Facts

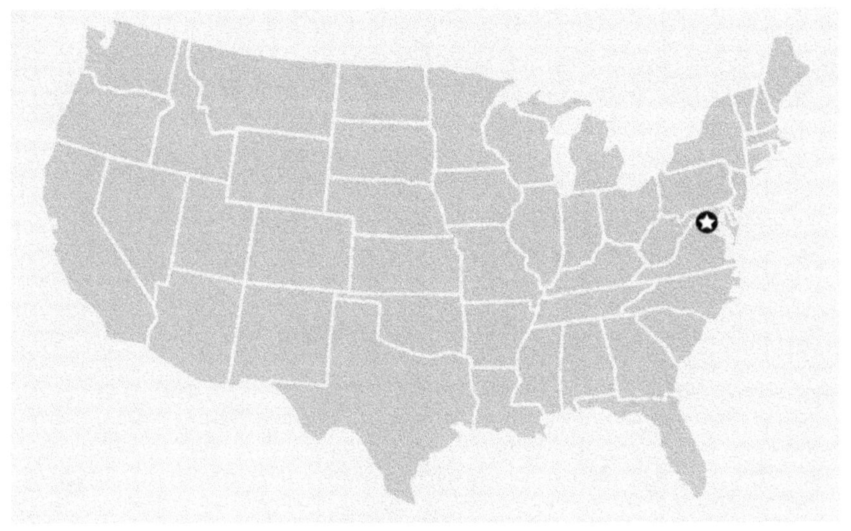

Home City

Washington, D.C.

Metro Area Population

About 6.4 Million

Home Arena

Capital One Arena

Arena Capacity

20,173

Conference / Division

Eastern Conference / Southeast Division

Famous Local Food

Half-smoke sausage, mumbo sauce, crab cakes, Ben's
Chili Bowl

Chapter 1: From Chicago to D.C. (The Origin Story)

1. Born in Chicago: The Packers, the Zephyrs, and a Very Confusing First Two Years

If you looked up the Washington Wizards in a history book and tried to trace their roots, you would end up in Chicago, staring at a team called the Packers. Not the Green Bay Packers. Not a moving company. The Chicago Packers, an NBA franchise named after the city's meatpacking industry. Yes, the first chapter of Washington Wizards history smells faintly like a butcher shop, and nobody can take that away.

The team was born in 1961 as an expansion franchise, which is a fancy way of saying the NBA basically said "fine, Chicago, you can have a team too." They finished their first season with a record of 18 wins and 62 losses, which is the basketball equivalent of showing up to a spelling bee and misspelling your own name. The franchise, to its credit, recognized this was not a great start.

So they changed the name. One year in, they scrapped "Packers" and became the Chicago Zephyrs, which sounds like a team that plays exclusively in breezy weather. The Zephyrs were also not very good. They went 25 and 55. Two names, two seasons, zero playoff appearances, and a city full of Chicagoans who were not particularly convinced they needed this team around. Chicago would not get its beloved Bulls until 1966, and even then, nobody was losing sleep over a franchise that could not win a third of its games. The Zephyrs read the room and did the only logical thing: they left.

2. The Baltimore Bullets: A New City, a New Identity

In 1963, the franchise packed up and moved to Baltimore, where they adopted one of the most famous names in NBA history: the Bullets. Baltimore already had a storied connection to that name. A different Baltimore Bullets team had won an NBA title all the way back in 1948, so the new franchise was essentially borrowing a legacy and hoping some of it would rub off. Historically speaking, this is a completely reasonable strategy.

The origin of the Bullets name has been debated for years. Some say it traces back to the ammunition factories that once operated in the Baltimore area. Others connect it to the old nickname for Baltimore itself. Whatever the true origin, the name stuck, and the team slowly started becoming something worth watching. They were not championship contenders yet, but they were building a roster with real talent, real attitude, and a city that finally seemed interested in keeping them around.

Imagine this: you are a basketball fan in Baltimore in the mid-1960s, watching this franchise find its footing for the first time. Nobody has heard of most of these players yet. The arena is loud and a little rough around the edges. Nobody knows that within a decade, this team will have one of the most iconic players in NBA history wearing their jersey. Right now it just feels like a team trying to figure out who it is. Which, honestly, is relatable.

3. Moving to the Capital: How Washington Got Its Team

The Bullets did not arrive in Washington all at once. It was more of a slow migration, the kind where you half-move and keep one foot in the old city while testing the waters in the new one. From 1963 to 1973, they played in Baltimore and built something real, reaching the Finals once before and once after the move. Then, in the 1973-74 season, they officially relocated to the D.C. area and briefly played as the Capital Bullets, which sounds like a team that could only exist inside the Beltway.

The move made sense geographically. Washington D.C. is the capital of the United States, home to millions of people, and the kind of city where being seen matters. Having a major NBA franchise planted in the middle of all that power and politics gave the team a new energy. They dropped the "Capital" and became the Washington Bullets, which had a harder, more confident sound to it.

What made the timing even better was that the roster was quietly becoming spectacular. A center named Wes Unseld was already one of the most respected players in the entire league, and a forward named Elvin Hayes had joined him to form one of the most physically dominant frontcourts anyone had seen. Washington did not just get a team. Washington got a team that was about to do something memorable, and we will get to that in Chapter 3.

4. The Name Change That Took Years: From Bullets to Wizards

By the 1990s, Washington D.C. was dealing with a genuine crisis. Gun violence in the city was at devastating levels, and the team's owner, Abe Pollin, felt deeply uncomfortable with his franchise being called the Bullets. Pollin had lost a close friend to gun violence, and he made a decision that almost no owner in professional sports had ever made before: he changed the team's name for moral reasons, not marketing ones.

In 1997, the Washington Bullets officially became the Washington Wizards. The reaction was... mixed. Some fans loved it. Some fans thought "Wizards" sounded like a fantasy novel, not an NBA franchise. Players were skeptical. Commentators debated it endlessly. One prominent player at the time reportedly said that the word "Bullets" never meant anything negative to him, and that changing it felt like erasing history. The debate has honestly never fully stopped.

But here is the thing about Abe Pollin's decision: it was genuine. He was not chasing a rebrand trend or trying to sell more jerseys. He genuinely believed the name was doing harm in a city that was already hurting. You can disagree with the call, and plenty of people do, but the intention was real. Today the Wizards name has had nearly thirty years to build its own legacy. Whether it has fully earned its place in the history books is a question Wizards fans have very strong opinions about. At family dinners. Loudly.

5. Capital One Arena: The House in the Heart of D.C.

Capital One Arena opened in 1997, the same year the team changed its name, which means the Wizards essentially launched two new identities at once and hoped for the best. The arena sits in the Penn Quarter neighborhood, right in the middle of downtown Washington D.C., which makes it one of the most centrally located NBA arenas in the entire country. You can walk out of a game and be standing next to a federal building before your ears stop ringing.

The arena has gone through a few name changes of its own over the years, starting as the MCI Center, then becoming the Verizon Center, and eventually landing on Capital One Arena when the bank paid for naming rights. It holds just over 20,000 fans for basketball, which means on a packed night it sounds like a very motivated small country inside a single building. The arena also hosts the Washington Capitals hockey team, concerts, college basketball, and occasionally whatever else the city needs a giant indoor venue for.

What makes the arena special for Wizards fans is its location. It is not tucked away in a suburb somewhere, hidden behind parking lots and highway exits. It is right there, in the city, part of the neighborhood, part of the noise. On game nights, the streets around it fill up with people in red and blue, arguing about lineup decisions and eating half a soft pretzel while walking. If you are going to be a team in the nation's capital, that is exactly where your building should be. Dead center and impossible to ignore.

6. Wes Unseld: The Immovable Object (1968-1981)

Wes Unseld was a 6-foot-7 center from Louisville, Kentucky, who showed up in Washington in 1968 and immediately made everyone else on the court feel like they had wandered into the wrong building. He was not the tallest center in the league. He was not the flashiest. He did not dazzle anyone with spin moves or post footwork that belonged in a highlight reel. What he did was set bone-rattling screens, grab every rebound that came within three feet of him, and play defense the way a brick wall plays defense. Immovable. Unpleasant. Extremely effective.

His teammates loved him. Opposing players respected him. Opposing players who tried to drive the lane also frequently needed a moment to collect themselves afterward. He did not need to score forty points a night to dominate a game. He just needed to show up, which he did, every single night, for thirteen seasons. Unseld was the kind of player who made everyone around him better simply by existing on the same floor, and the Bullets were a completely different team with him in the middle than they were without him.

What Unseld accomplished in his very first NBA season was so historically remarkable that it deserves its own spotlight, and we will give it exactly that in Fact 13. Consider this your warning that it is coming and it is going to make your jaw drop.

7. Elvin Hayes: The Big E (1972-1981)

Elvin Hayes arrived in Washington via trade in 1972, and the Bullets suddenly had something genuinely terrifying in their frontcourt. Hayes was 6-foot-9, could score from almost anywhere, and had a turnaround jumper so smooth it looked like it belonged in a completely different sport. His nickname was "The Big E," which is exactly what you name a player when you run out of words to describe how dominant he is and just start pointing.

Hayes had already made himself famous before he got to Washington. As a college player at the University of Houston, he was part of one of the most hyped college basketball games in history, a nationally televised showdown against Lew Alcindor, who you may know better as Kareem Abdul-Jabbar. Hayes dropped 39 points in that game and Houston won. He arrived in the

NBA already carrying legend status, which is a very good thing to carry.

Pairing Hayes with Wes Unseld gave the Bullets a frontcourt that the rest of the Eastern Conference had serious nightmares about. Two enormous, physical, relentless players who absolutely refused to be moved. Imagine trying to score against both of them in the same possession. Imagine trying to rebound over either of them. Now imagine trying to do both. That is what opponents faced every single night, and it is a large part of the reason why, by the mid-1970s, Washington was no longer a team people slept on. They were a team people actively prepared for, stressed about, and occasionally just hoped would lose before they had to face them.

Elvin Hayes powering through the paint for the Washington Bullets in the 1970s. Tough rebounds. Strong post moves. "The Big E" helped lead the franchise to its 1978 NBA championship. *Photo: Elvin Hayes with the*

8. Earl Monroe: The Pearl (1967-1971)

Before Earl Monroe became a New York Knick and a basketball legend of a different borough, he spent his early career in Baltimore making crowds absolutely lose their minds. Monroe played for the Bullets from 1967 to 1971 and in that short window established himself as one of the most genuinely thrilling players the sport had ever seen. His nickname was "The Pearl," and if you saw him play, you understood immediately why nobody argued about it.

Monroe's game was built on improvisation. He spun, he hesitated, he changed direction mid-move in ways that left defenders looking like they had just tried to chase a hummingbird. He did not run set plays so much as he created small pieces of magic in real time, each one slightly different from the last, none of them something you could have drawn up on a whiteboard. Coaches probably watched him and felt both thrilled and mildly terrified.

In his very first NBA season, Monroe averaged over 24 points per game and won Rookie of the Year. The city of Baltimore went absolutely wild for him, and for good reason. He was not just a good player. He was a personality, a style, a vibe that made every single game feel like something might happen that nobody had ever seen before. When he was eventually traded to the Knicks in 1971, Baltimore fans were heartbroken in that specific way that only happens when you realize you had something special and it is now someone else's problem to appreciate. The Pearl left Baltimore, but Baltimore never quite got over it.

9. Gilbert Arenas: Agent Zero (2003-2010)

Gilbert Arenas is one of the most fascinating players in NBA history, and the fact that he is not brought up in every single "most entertaining players ever" conversation is a genuine injustice. Arenas came to Washington in 2003 after being passed over in the draft by teams that apparently did not realize they were passing over Gilbert Arenas. He wore number zero because, as he explained, every team that had the chance to draft him gave him a big fat zero. He then proceeded to become an All-Star three times and score more points than most of the people who passed on him ever dreamed of. Nothing motivates a person quite like being told they are not good enough.

At his peak, Arenas was one of the most dangerous scorers in basketball. He could create his own shot from anywhere, had a mid-range game that was basically unstoppable, and played with a confidence that occasionally crossed into territory that could only be described as gloriously unhinged. He once made a three-pointer to win a game and then stood at half-court pretending to blow out imaginary candles on an imaginary birthday cake. This was just a normal Tuesday for Agent Zero.

The Wizards teams of the mid-2000s, with Arenas alongside Antawn Jamison and Caron Butler, were one of the most fun groups in the entire NBA. They made the playoffs multiple times. They pushed the Cleveland Cavaliers, featuring a young LeBron James, to six hard games in 2006. Arenas put up 32 points in a playoff game against the Cavs after playing on a bad knee and basically announced his presence to the entire basketball world at once. Washington has not always been easy to love as a basketball city, but those Arenas years? Those were genuinely, undeniably worth watching.

10. John Wall and Bradley Beal: The Dream Backcourt (2012-2019)

In 2010, the Washington Wizards won the NBA Draft Lottery, which felt like the universe finally deciding to give D.C. fans a break. With the first overall pick, they selected John Wall out of Kentucky, a point guard so fast that opposing coaches reportedly watched film of him and then just sat quietly for a while. Wall was electric. He could get from half-court to the basket in what felt like approximately two seconds, and his handle was so good it seemed unfair to everyone who had spent years practicing basketball the normal way.

Two years later, Washington drafted Bradley Beal with the third overall pick, and suddenly the Wizards had something they had not had in a long time: a reason for genuine optimism. Beal was a shooting guard with a smooth jumper, a competitive streak, and the kind of reliability that Wall's explosiveness needed beside it. Together they became one of the most exciting young backcourts in the league, and for a few seasons in the mid-2010s, the city of Washington allowed itself to believe this might actually be the beginning of something special.

They made the playoffs multiple times. They pushed the Boston Celtics to seven games in 2017 in a series that had the whole city holding its breath. Wall made the All-Star team five times. Beal became one of the most consistent scorers in the entire NBA. The partnership was real, the talent was real, and the hope was very, very real. What came next is a longer story involving injuries and roster moves that we will get into later. But for a window of time, the Wall and Beal era had Washington buzzing in a way the city had not experienced since the days of Agent Zero blowing out imaginary candles on an imaginary cake.

11. The 1978 NBA Championship: How Washington Won It All

The 1978 NBA Finals between the Washington Bullets and the Seattle SuperSonics is one of the most dramatic championship series in league history, and it deserves way more attention than it gets at Thanksgiving dinner tables across America. The series went back and forth like two teams that genuinely could not decide who wanted it more. Washington would grab momentum, Seattle would take it right back. Nobody was comfortable. Nobody was safe. Every game felt like it could go either way, and several of them basically did.

Wes Unseld was the engine of the whole thing. He grabbed rebounds like a man who had been personally offended by the basketball touching anyone else. He set screens that defensive players described later in tones usually reserved for natural disasters. When the series reached Game 7 with everything on the line, Washington went to Seattle and did something the Bullets franchise had never done before: they won a championship on the road, in hostile territory, in front of a crowd that desperately wanted them to fail. They did not fail. They won 105-99 and brought the trophy back to D.C.

When the final buzzer sounded, Washington had its first and only NBA championship. Unseld won Finals MVP, which he absolutely deserved, and the city of D.C. erupted in the kind of celebration that only happens when a team wins something genuinely hard-fought and genuinely earned. For Wizards fans today, 1978 is the year. It is the number they carry everywhere. It is also, unfortunately, the last time they have needed to buy championship merchandise, but we will politely move past that for now.

12. The 1979 Repeat Run: Almost Back-to-Back

Fresh off their 1978 championship, the Washington Bullets came back the very next season and made it all the way to the NBA Finals again, which is the kind of thing that makes a city think it has figured something out. Back-to-back championships are extraordinarily rare in the NBA. Only a handful of franchises have ever done it. Washington was one win away from joining that list, and then Seattle happened again.

The 1979 Finals was a rematch of the year before, and this time the SuperSonics were ready. They had studied the Bullets, adjusted their approach, and came out with a hunger that Washington simply could not match. Seattle won the series four games to one, claiming the championship that Washington had been carrying in its back pocket since June. It was a painful loss, the specific kind that stings more than a regular loss because you know how close you were. You had already won it once. You could almost taste the second one.

Pretend for a minute you are a Bullets fan in 1979, sitting in the arena watching Seattle celebrate on your home floor. You know your team just won a championship twelve months ago. You know they fought all the way back to the Finals. You are watching the trophy go to someone else by the thinnest possible margin of effort and momentum. That feeling, right there, is the purest and most frustrating thing about sports. Washington has spent a lot of years chasing that feeling again. The chase continues.

13. The Rookie Season That Nobody Has Ever Matched

In the entire history of the NBA, only two players have ever won Rookie of the Year and Most Valuable Player in the same season. Wes Unseld was one of them.

He won NBA Rookie of the Year and NBA Most Valuable Player in his first season. One year in the league. Brand new. Still learning where the visitor locker rooms were. MVP of the entire sport.

To understand how absurd this is, consider that the MVP award almost always goes to an established superstar who has spent years building a reputation, accumulating statistics, and earning the respect of every voter in the league. Rookie of the Year goes to the best first-year player. Winning both in the same year is like showing up to your first day of high school and being voted class president, homecoming king, and most likely to succeed simultaneously. It does not happen. Except it happened to Wes Unseld, who apparently did not get the memo that you were supposed to ease into things.

The only other player in NBA history to win both awards in the same season was Wilt Chamberlain, which tells you everything you need to know about the company Unseld was keeping. Chamberlain is widely considered one of the two or three greatest players who ever lived. Unseld belongs in that same sentence when people are talking about the greatest Bullets and Wizards of all time. The 1969 season was not just a great rookie year. It was one of the most statistically and historically remarkable debuts in the entire history of professional basketball, and it announced to the whole league that Washington had something genuinely special.

14. The 2017 Playoffs: When Wall and Beal Made Everyone Nervous

The 2017 NBA Playoffs will not go down as Washington's greatest postseason run. They did not win the championship. They did not even make the conference finals. But what they did do was take the Boston Celtics, one of the best teams in the Eastern Conference that year, all the way to Game 7 of the second round, and they did it in a way that had the entire basketball world paying attention to D.C. for the first time in years.

John Wall was otherworldly in that series. He attacked Boston's defense repeatedly, got to the basket at will, and made clutch plays in moments where lesser players disappear into the background and pretend to be busy. Bradley Beal shot the ball with the kind of confidence you only see from players who have genuinely stopped worrying about missing. The two of them together looked, for a few games, like exactly the kind of backcourt that could carry a franchise to a championship someday. The Garden in Boston got very quiet during a couple of those games, which is not a thing that happens easily.

Game 7 ended with Boston winning and Washington going home, which is how most Washington sports stories end and why D.C. fans have the emotional endurance of people who have been training for disappointment their whole lives. But the 2017 run mattered because it proved Wall and Beal were real. Not almost-real. Not kind-of-real on a good night. Actually, genuinely, worth-building-around real. The city believed in them after that series. Whether the front office did enough with that belief is a whole separate chapter, and also a whole separate therapy session.

15. The Night Agent Zero Went for 60

On January 14, 2006, Gilbert Arenas walked into the Staples Center in Los Angeles, looked at the Lakers, and decided that 60 points sounded like a reasonable evening's work. Arenas poured in 60 points against Los Angeles in a performance so ludicrous that even Lakers fans, who were rooting against him, had to stop and acknowledge what they were watching. It was one of the highest-scoring individual games in Washington franchise history, and it came from a player who had been told, multiple times, by multiple teams, that he was not good enough to be in the league at all.

The thing about Arenas that made performances like this so delightful was the attitude he brought to every single one of them. He was not serious about his own greatness in the way some scorers are, all furrowed brows and post-game speeches about the process. Arenas was having fun. He played basketball the way a kid plays basketball in the driveway when nobody is watching, except the driveway was a professional NBA arena and 20,000 people were watching and he was doing it against actual NBA defenders. He was genuinely, infectiously, sometimes ridiculously entertaining.

Sixty points in one game is a number that puts you in very rare company. Most NBA players never score 60 in their entire career all at once. Arenas did it on a random January Saturday against the Lakers and then probably went home and posted something chaotic on the internet about it, because that was entirely his brand. For Wizards fans, the 60-point game is one of those moments you keep in your back pocket to pull out whenever someone tries to tell you that Washington has never had a truly special player. You just smile, say Gilbert Arenas, sixty points, Lakers, 2006, and then walk away slowly. It is very effective.

Chapter 4: Traditions, Mascots, and the Wildest Facts in the District

16. G-Wiz: The Mascot Who Has Seen Everything

G-Wiz, the official mascot of the Washington Wizards, is a large fuzzy creature of indeterminate species wearing a Wizards uniform and radiating the specific energy of someone who has been doing this job for nearly thirty years and has absolutely no intention of stopping. He was introduced in 1997, the same year the team changed its name from the Bullets to the Wizards, which means G-Wiz and the Wizards identity were essentially born on the same day. They grew up together. That is either heartwarming or slightly chaotic depending on your perspective.

Nobody is entirely sure what G-Wiz is supposed to be, which is part of his charm. He looks like a dark blue flightless raven with a red wizard hat, gold stars on his gloves, and enormous eyes that suggest he has seen things. Washington Wizards players themselves have been asked what G-Wiz is and have responded with answers including "a big blue Christmas tree," "a mix of a Teletubby and Cookie Monster," and "Bigfoot disguised as a superhero." The players live and work with this creature regularly. They still cannot identify him. This tells you everything you need to know about G-Wiz's commitment to mystery.

G-Wiz has outlasted coaches, general managers, entire rosters of players, and at least four complete rebuilds of the franchise. Through all of it he has remained cheerful, relentless, deeply fuzzy, and absolutely essential to the game-night experience. He has his own fan base, his own social media presence, and a jersey number of 00, which is very on brand for a mascot who defies easy categorization. Every franchise needs a constant. Washington's constant is a blue creature of unknown origin who can dunk on a trampoline and has been doing so since the Clinton administration.

17. The Name Debate: Why Some Fans Still Call Them the Bullets

Nearly thirty years after the name change, there are still Washington fans who call the team the Bullets. Not out of disrespect for the reasons behind the switch. Not because they do not know it happened. Simply because some identities dig so deep into a city's bones that no official rebrand can fully uproot them. The Bullets name represented something raw and real about Baltimore and Washington for three decades, and a lot of longtime fans are not ready to let it go, which is honestly very on-brand for a city that also still argues about which half-smoke stand is the best one.

The debate comes up every few years when a journalist writes a piece about it, or when a particularly nostalgic fan puts on an old throwback jersey and gets a reaction at the arena. Some people think the Wizards name has never quite fit the franchise, that it sounds more like a minor league team from a city that really loves magic shows than a serious NBA contender. Others have fully embraced it, pointing out that the Wizards brand has now existed longer than the Bullets brand did in Washington. Time, it turns out, is the most powerful rebrand tool available.

What everyone agrees on is that Abe Pollin deserves respect regardless of where you land on the name itself. The Bullets era gave Washington championships, legends, and decades of memories. The Wizards era gave Washington Gilbert Arenas, John Wall, and a mascot who rides tiny bikes. Both eras have their merits. You are allowed to love both. You are also allowed to have a very loud opinion about it, and if you are in Washington, you probably already do.

18. The Curse of the Lottery: Washington's Draft History is a Rollercoaster

The Washington Wizards have held some very high draft picks over the years, which sounds like a great thing and sometimes actually is. In 2010 they took John Wall first overall and got exactly what they hoped for. In 2012 they took Bradley Beal third overall and got a future All-Star. These are the draft success stories, the ones Wizards fans frame on the wall and point to proudly. Then there are the others.

Washington has also made draft selections that were, to put it charitably, more educational than successful. The franchise has drafted players who never developed, players who were injured almost immediately, and players who were perfectly fine on other teams but never quite clicked in D.C., which is the most frustrating kind of wrong because you cannot even be properly mad about it. Over the years the Wizards have sat in draft lottery rooms full of hope and walked out with mixed results often enough that the lottery itself has become something Wizards fans watch through partially covered eyes, like a horror movie where you already know something bad is coming but you keep watching anyway.

The silver lining, and there genuinely is one, is that Washington has shown it can identify talent when the pieces fall right. Wall and Beal were not accidents. They were good scouting and good luck arriving at the same time. Every team in the league has draft misses. The Wizards just occasionally have them in spectacular fashion, which at least makes for good stories. Draft night in Washington is never boring. It is sometimes painful, occasionally thrilling, and almost always memorable for one reason or another.

19. The Presidents Race: The Greatest Halftime Show in Sports

At some point in the mid-1990s, someone at a Washington sports organization had an idea so gloriously unhinged that it has now become one of the most beloved traditions in American professional sports. That idea was this: what if we had giant foam-headed versions of the American presidents race each other around the field during the middle of a game? The idea started with the Washington Nationals baseball team, but the Presidents Race became such a defining piece of D.C. sports culture that it deserves a spot in this book, because it says everything you need to know about what kind of city Washington is.

The original racing presidents were George Washington, Thomas Jefferson, Abraham Lincoln, and Theodore Roosevelt. Roosevelt famously did not win for years and years, becoming a beloved underdog figure whose losing streak became its own running joke. Fans started showing up specifically to see whether Teddy would finally cross the line first. Teddy lost so many races that his futility became legendary. When he finally won, it was treated as a genuine sporting event. A foam-headed cartoon president crossing a finish line first made headlines. Washington is a special place.

The connection to the Wizards is that D.C. sports culture is one unified, slightly chaotic, intensely passionate thing, and the Presidents Race is one of its most perfect expressions. It is silly. It is local. It is completely unique to this city. No other sports market in America could have invented the Presidents Race because no other city has this particular combination of political history, civic pride, and willingness to put giant foam heads on people and call it entertainment. Washington owns this. It is wonderful.

20. Famous Wizards Fans, D.C. Connections, and Only-in-Washington Moments

Washington D.C. is the only city in America where you can look three rows up from courtside and spot a senator, a cabinet secretary, and a famous journalist all arguing about a foul call at the same time. The Wizards play in the nation's capital, which means their fan base includes some of the most powerful and recognizable people on the planet, all of whom apparently need somewhere to go on a Tuesday night when Congress is not in session.

Over the years Capital One Arena has hosted presidents, vice presidents, diplomats, celebrities, and an entire ecosystem of Washington insiders who spend their days running the country and their evenings yelling at referees like everyone else. There is something deeply humanizing about watching a senator stand up and pump his fist over a John Wall fast break, because in that moment he is not a senator. He is just a guy who really needed that basket. Basketball has a way of doing that to people regardless of their title.

The Wizards have also had their share of genuinely only-in-Washington moments over the years, from games that were attended by foreign dignitaries to partnerships with D.C. organizations doing real community work in the city. The franchise is woven into the fabric of the capital in a way that goes beyond just playing games there. They are part of what makes D.C. D.C., which is a city that somehow manages to be the center of the entire world and a fiercely local town at exactly the same time.

21. The Post-Wall Era: Rebuilding and Reloading

For years, John Wall and Bradley Beal were the identity of the Washington Wizards. Wall's explosiveness and Beal's scoring reliability gave the franchise something genuine to build around, and the city believed in them. Then came the injuries, the roster shuffles, and eventually the trades that ended both partnerships. Wall departed in a complicated exit that nobody came out of looking great. Beal, after years of loyalty through difficult seasons, was traded to the Phoenix Suns in 2023. Just like that, the era was over. D.C. sports fans know this feeling well. It does not get easier with practice.

What the Wizards were left with was a roster in full reset mode and a front office facing the kind of decisions that define franchises for the next decade. The comfortable option was to keep patching, keep adding veterans, keep pretending the team was closer than it actually was. Washington chose the harder path: acknowledge the rebuild, embrace it, and start building something sustainable from the ground up. This is the part of the process that requires the most patience from fans, because watching a team prioritize the future means watching a lot of games in the present that feel extremely low-stakes.

The post-Wall, post-Beal era is still being written. Young players are developing. Draft picks are arriving. Coaches and front office decision-makers are making the calls that will shape the next chapter of basketball in the nation's capital. It is not the most glamorous phase of franchise building. It is, however, a necessary one, and Washington has shown before that it can come out the other side with something worth cheering about. The city is patient. The city has earned that patience.

22. Kyle Kuzma and the Bridge Generation

Kyle Kuzma arrived in Washington as part of the Russell Westbrook trade in 2021, which is a sentence that contains more storylines than most novels. He came in relatively quietly, as players often do when they arrive in a trade involving names bigger than theirs, and then proceeded to become one of the most productive forwards in the entire NBA. Kuzma averaged over 21 points per game in his second season with Washington and turned himself into exactly the kind of player who makes other teams nervous when they see him on the schedule. He was not supposed to be the main character. He became one anyway.

What made Kuzma's development in Washington so satisfying was that it was genuinely unexpected. He had been a solid rotation player on championship-contending Lakers teams, good but not starring. In Washington he got the ball, got the minutes, and got the chance to show what he could actually do when the offense ran through him. He took that chance and ran with it, then dunked on someone, then hit a difficult mid-range jumper, then did it all again the next night. Sometimes players just need the right situation, and Washington turned out to be Kuzma's right situation in a way that surprised almost everyone except probably Kuzma himself.

Kuzma represented something important for the Wizards beyond just his statistics. He was proof that the franchise could still develop talent, still be a destination, still build something worth watching even during a period when the expectations were being recalibrated. He was not the final answer to Washington's rebuild. He was more like a very encouraging sign that the pieces were starting to come together, which after a few rough years is exactly the kind of sign a fan base needs to stay interested.

23. The Draft Reset: Washington's Bet on the Future

At some point every rebuilding team has to commit. They have to stop being halfway between competing and rebuilding, stop adding veterans to appease the present while also hoarding picks for the future, and just decide which direction they are actually going. Washington made that decision, and it involved accumulating draft picks with the enthusiasm of someone who just discovered that draft picks are free and the warehouse has no closing time.

The Wizards began stockpiling future selections and young players, betting that building through the draft was the most sustainable path back to relevance. This is the part of the rebuilding process that requires the most patience from fans, because watching a team prioritize the future means watching a team play a lot of games in the present that are heavy on effort and light on wins. The record suffers. The standings are not pretty. The highlight reels are shorter. But the asset base grows, and the eventual payoff, when it comes, tends to be worth the wait.

Washington's fans have seen this movie before. They watched Wall develop from a lottery pick into an All-Star. They watched Beal grow from a promising young guard into one of the most reliable scorers in the league. The franchise has shown it can identify and develop talent when everything aligns. The draft reset is essentially a bet that they can do it again, with new names and a new supporting cast. Whether that bet pays off is the central question hanging over the franchise, and the answer is currently being written one draft pick at a time.

24. Capital One Arena and the Modern Fan Experience

Capital One Arena in 2025 is a very different building from the one that opened in 1997, and not just because it has a different bank's name on the outside. The arena has been renovated and upgraded repeatedly over the years, adding technology, improving amenities, and generally trying to make the experience of watching basketball there feel like something you would actually choose to do over staying home on your couch, which is a genuinely competitive challenge in the modern sports landscape.

The arena's downtown location remains its single greatest asset. You can take the Metro directly to a game, which in a city famous for traffic is not a minor convenience, it is practically a public service. You walk out of the subway station and the arena is right there, surrounded by restaurants and bars that fill up before tip-off with fans in red and blue having the kind of pre-game conversations that sound extremely confident and occasionally turn out to be completely wrong. It is one of the best pre-game atmospheres in the league, built entirely on geography and the specific energy of a city that takes everything, including basketball, seriously.

The Wizards have also invested in the game-night experience itself, with entertainment, promotions, and fan engagement programs designed to make every visit memorable even when the team is in a rebuilding phase. This matters more than casual fans realize. A franchise that treats its fans well during the hard years earns loyalty that pays off enormously during the good years. Washington has had enough hard years to understand this deeply, and Capital One Arena on a good night, with a full crowd and something on the line, is still one of the better places in the NBA to watch basketball.

25. What It Means to Be a Wizards Fan Today

Being a Washington Wizards fan in 2025 requires a very specific personality type. You need enough optimism to keep showing up, enough historical knowledge to appreciate what this franchise has actually accomplished, enough humor to survive the stretches where things do not go according to plan, and enough loyalty to stick around when the rebuilding process makes the standings look like a cry for help. It is not the easiest fan experience in the league. It is also not the worst, and Wizards fans will tell you that with the particular pride of people who have earned their perspective.

The Wizards gave Washington its only NBA championship in 1978, a fact that deserves more celebration than it gets. They gave the city Wes Unseld, one of the most uniquely impactful players in league history. They gave it Earl Monroe spinning past defenders in Baltimore. They gave it Gilbert Arenas scoring 60 in Los Angeles and then probably posting about it online. They gave it John Wall flying down the court at a speed that made physics seem optional. They gave it Bradley Beal, consistent and excellent and present through all of it. That is a real legacy. That is worth something.

The future of the Wizards is genuinely open right now, which is either exciting or terrifying depending on your disposition. A young roster is developing. Draft picks are arriving. Coaches and front office people are making decisions that will shape the next decade of basketball in the nation's capital. Somewhere in there is the next player who will make D.C. fans lose their minds, the next moment that will end up in a book like this one, the next reason to stand up in Capital One Arena and scream at the top of your lungs. The history is great. The story is still being written. And if you are a Wizards fan, you would not want it any other way.

Bonus Trivia Quiz!

You think you are a true Wizards fan? Try this bonus quiz!

1. The Washington Wizards franchise began in 1961 under what name?

A) The Washington Warriors
B) The Chicago Packers
C) The Baltimore Bullets
D) The Capital Zephyrs

2. Which city did the franchise play in BEFORE moving to the Washington D.C. area?

A) Philadelphia
B) Detroit
C) Baltimore
D) Cleveland

3. Why did owner Abe Pollin change the team name from Bullets to Wizards in 1997?

A) A new sponsor required the name change
B) The players voted for a new identity
C) He felt the name was harmful given gun violence in the city
D) The original Bullets trademark expired

4. Capital One Arena is located in which Washington D.C. neighborhood?

A) Georgetown
B) Dupont Circle
C) Penn Quarter
D) Adams Morgan

5. Wes Unseld was only the second player in NBA history to win Rookie of the Year AND MVP in the same season. Who was the first?

A) Bill Russell
B) Oscar Robertson
C) Jerry West
D) Wilt Chamberlain

6. Elvin Hayes got the nickname "The Big E" and came to Washington via trade in 1972. What college did he famously play for before the NBA?

A) UCLA
B) University of Houston
C) Kentucky
D) Duke

7. Earl "The Pearl" Monroe was traded away from the Bullets in 1971. Which team did he join?

A) Boston Celtics
B) Los Angeles Lakers
C) New York Knicks
D) Chicago Bulls

8. Gilbert Arenas wore number zero for the Wizards. Why did he choose that number?

A) His favorite player growing up wore zero
B) Every team that could have drafted him passed on him
C) Zero was the only number available when he signed
D) He wanted to stand out from other players

9. How many points did Gilbert Arenas score against the Los Angeles Lakers on January 14, 2006?

A) 51
B) 55
C) 58
D) 60

10. The Washington Bullets won their only NBA Championship in what year?

A) 1974

B) 1976

C) 1978

D) 1980

11. The Bullets made it back to the NBA Finals the very next year in 1979. Who beat them to win the championship?

A) Boston Celtics

B) Seattle SuperSonics

C) Portland Trail Blazers

D) Phoenix Suns

12. In the 2017 playoffs, John Wall and Bradley Beal pushed which team all the way to Game 7 before being eliminated?

A) Cleveland Cavaliers

B) Toronto Raptors

C) Boston Celtics

D) Miami Heat

13. What is the name of the Washington Wizards official mascot?

A) Wiz Kid

B) G-Wiz

C) Wizzy

D) Capital W

14. John Wall was selected with what pick in the 2010 NBA Draft?

A) First overall

B) Second overall

C) Third overall

D) Fifth overall

15. Kyle Kuzma arrived in Washington as part of a trade involving which high-profile player?

A) John Wall

B) Bradley Beal

C) Russell Westbrook

D) Carmelo Anthony

Only a true Wizards fan will know this.

(No Answer Provided)

In Wes Unseld's legendary 1968-69 MVP season, his points per game average was remarkably modest for an MVP winner. Which of the following is closest to his actual scoring average that season?

A) 10.5 points per game
B) 13.8 points per game
C) 17.2 points per game
D) 20.9 points per game

Answer Key

1. B) The Chicago Packers

2. C) Baltimore

3. C) He felt the name was harmful given gun violence in the city

4. C) Penn Quarter

5. D) Wilt Chamberlain

6. B) University of Houston

7. C) New York Knicks

8. B) Every team that could have drafted him passed on him

9. D) 60

10. C) 1978

11. B) Seattle SuperSonics

12. C) Boston Celtics

13. B) G-Wiz

14. A) First overall

15. C) Russell Westbrook

NBA PLAYOFF BRACKET

* Fill in your picks and try not to argue with your friends about it!

Part of the Fun Fan Facts: The Unofficial Sports Guide Series

Be the Boss of the Playoffs

You've broken down the matchups. You know which superstar takes over in the fourth quarter. You've seen the bench units that quietly decide series. You've watched the adjustments coaches make when their backs are against the wall.

Now it's time to stop watching and start deciding.

On this page, you are not just a fan. You are the Head Coach drawing up the last play with three seconds left on the clock. You are the GM who built this roster. You are the analyst who saw it all coming.

This is not just filling out a bracket.

This is building your championship run.

Sixteen teams enter the NBA Playoffs. The path is brutal. Best of seven. No shortcuts. No hiding. Every round gets louder, harder, and more personal.

This bracket is your Playoff Control Room.

The Game Plan

1. Survive Round One: Start with the opening round. Which matchup is going seven games? Who has the closer? Who folds under pressure? Make the calls.

2. Feel the Momentum: As you move into the Conference Semifinals and Conference Finals, things change. Role players become heroes. Stars feel the weight. Trust your reads.

3. Own the Finals: Trace your picks all the way to the NBA Finals. When the confetti falls and the trophy is raised, you'll find out who earned it.

House Rules: Circle your boldest upset. That is your official "I knew it" moment.

Choose Your Weapon: Pencil if you want flexibility. Pen if you trust your instincts. Sharpie if you believe in chaos.

Because once the playoffs tip off, there is no rewinding Game 7.

Make your picks. Trust your basketball brain. And let the playoff drama begin.

Fun Facts Wrap-Up

You made it through! You're officially a true superfan! Now it's time to put your knowledge to the test. Share these facts with friends and see who really knows their team best.

Love the series?

Your reviews help other fans discover Fun Fan Facts. If you enjoyed this book, we'd really appreciate you sharing your thoughts and leaving a review.

Want more Fun Fan Facts?

Scan the QR code below to visit our site and explore bonus trivia, challenges, and special extras - including new teams, future series, and collectible fun as they're released.

Collect All the Fun Fan Facts Series!

Check off every book you read. See the full set on Amazon. Search "Fun Fan Facts Jake Liam."

World Cup 2026 Edition

☐ Algeria   ☐ Scotland   ☐ Morocco
☐ France   ☐ Brazil   ☐ Switzerland
☐ Paraguay   ☐ Ivory Coast   ☐ Curaçao
☐ Argentina   ☐ Senegal   ☐ Netherlands
☐ Germany   ☐ Canada   ☐ Tunisia
☐ Portugal   ☐ Japan   ☐ Ecuador
☐ Australia   ☐ South Africa   ☐ New Zealand
☐ Ghana   ☐ Cape Verde   ☐ United States
☐ Qatar   ☐ Jordan   ☐ Egypt
☐ Austria   ☐ South Korea   ☐ Norway
☐ Haiti   ☐ Colombia   ☐ Uruguay
☐ Saudi Arabia   ☐ Mexico   ☐ England
☐ Belgium   ☐ Spain   ☐ Panama
☐ Iran   ☐ Croatia   ☐ Uzbekistan

World Cup 2026 Group Edition

☐ Group A   ☐ Group F   ☐ Group K
☐ Group E   ☐ Group J   ☐ Group D
☐ Group I   ☐ Group C   ☐ Group H
☐ Group B   ☐ Group G   ☐ Group L

English Football Edition

☐ Arsenal F.C.

☐ Aston Villa F.C.

☐ Chelsea F.C.

☐ Everton F.C.

☐ Fulham F.C.

☐ Liverpool F.C.

☐ Manchester City

☐ Manchester United

☐ Newcastle United F.C.

☐ Tottenham Hotspur

☐ West Ham United

☐ Wrexham A.F.C.

NBA Edition

☐ Atlanta Hawks

☐ Boston Celtics

☐ Brooklyn Nets

☐ Charlotte Hornets

☐ Chicago Bulls

☐ Cleveland Cavaliers

☐ Dallas Mavericks

☐ Denver Nuggets

☐ Detroit Pistons

☐ Golden State Warriors

☐ Houston Rockets

☐ Indiana Pacers

☐ LA Clippers

☐ Los Angeles Lakers

☐ Memphis Grizzlies

☐ Miami Heat

☐ Milwaukee Bucks

☐ Minnesota Timberwolves

☐ New Orleans Pelicans

☐ New York Knicks

☐ Oklahoma City Thunder

☐ Orlando Magic

☐ Philadelphia 76ers

☐ Phoenix Suns

☐ Portland Trail Blazers

☐ Sacramento Kings

☐ San Antonio Spurs

☐ Toronto Raptors

☐ Utah Jazz

☐ Washington Wizards

About the Author

Jake is a 13-year-old sports fan who loves football, American football, and basketball. He plays soccer as a goalie and dreams of one day playing for West Ham United and helping teach kids to love the game. His passion for sports runs in the family - his dad was a professional baseball player, and his stepdad sparked his love for West Ham. Through the Fun Fan Facts series, he shares the fun and excitement of sports with fans everywhere.